The TOOTH Book

A GUIDE to HEALTHY TEETH and GUMS

Edward Miller

Holiday House / New York

How would it be to have no teeth? It wouldn't be much fun. Without teeth it's hard to eat, talk, smile, whistle, and sing.

Many animals have teeth too.

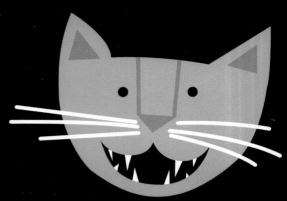

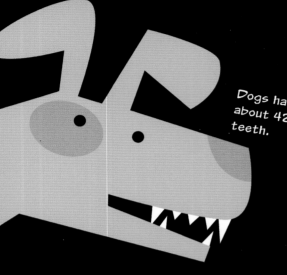

Dogs have about 42 teeth.

Cats have about 30 teeth.

Rodents' front teeth never stop growing, so they gnaw on wood to trim them down.

When a crocodile's mouth is closed, its teeth are on the outside.

Horses have very long teeth that grow continually.

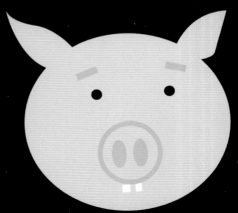

Pigs have about 44 teeth.

Wild pigs dig with specialized teeth, called tusks.

Elephants have the largest tusks.

Many snakes use their teeth to kill their prey. They swallow their victims whole.

Walruses use their tusks to hold onto ice while they are sleeping.

Hey, ducks don't have teeth!

QUACK!

TOOTH

0   6 months   2 ½ years

Primary teeth start forming before a baby is even born.

When a baby is around 6 months old primary teeth will start pushing through the gums. The 2 bottom center teeth usually come in first.

Between ages 6 months and 2 ½ years a baby's primary teeth will grow in. Most babies will have 20 primary teeth.

You will have 2 sets of teeth in your lifetime. The first set is called your **PRIMARY TEETH,** or baby teeth.

TIMELINE

By age 6 or 7 a kid will have usually lost his or her first primary tooth.

Between 6 and 13 years old a kid's permanent teeth will grow in.

Between ages 17 and 21 the last 4 teeth grow in—adding up to 32 permanent teeth in all.

The second set is your **PERMANENT TEETH**, which you will have your whole life—but only if you take good care of them.

SEE inside a TOOTH →

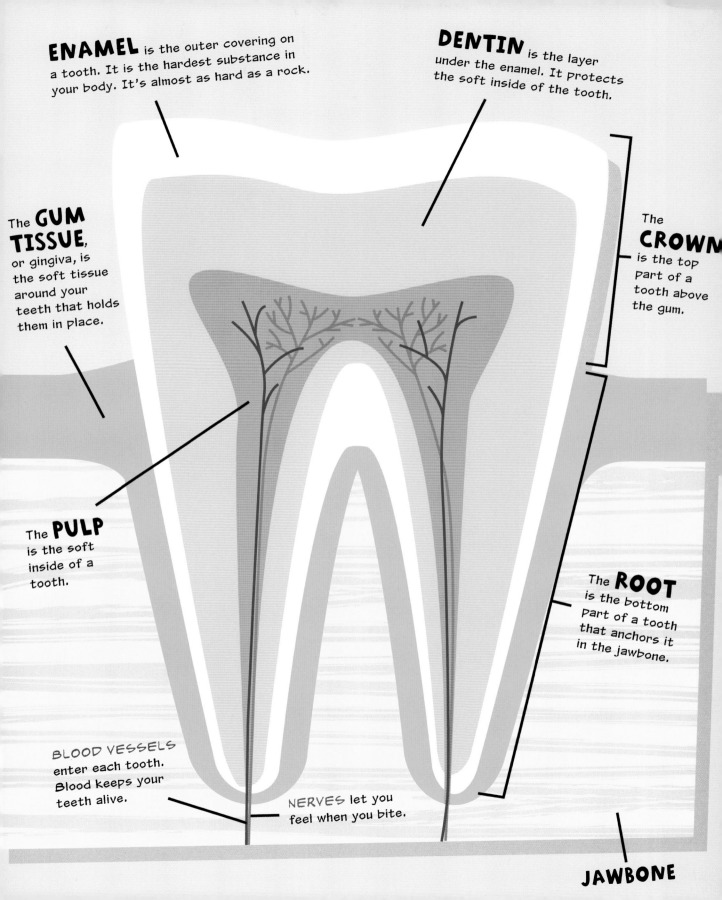

ENAMEL is the outer covering on a tooth. It is the hardest substance in your body. It's almost as hard as a rock.

DENTIN is the layer under the enamel. It protects the soft inside of the tooth.

The **GUM TISSUE**, or gingiva, is the soft tissue around your teeth that holds them in place.

The **CROWN** is the top part of a tooth above the gum.

The **PULP** is the soft inside of a tooth.

The **ROOT** is the bottom part of a tooth that anchors it in the jawbone.

BLOOD VESSELS enter each tooth. Blood keeps your teeth alive.

NERVES let you feel when you bite.

JAWBONE

LOST TOOTH

When kids are around 6 years old their primary teeth start to fall out—one by one—until they are all gone by about age 13. As one tooth falls out a permanent tooth grows in its place. Most kids find losing a tooth scary, but it's truly painless if the tooth is ready to come out. The spot where the tooth comes out may bleed, but you can stop the bleeding quickly with a small piece of tissue. Losing a tooth can actually be an exciting experience.

In countries such as Greece, India, and China, kids throw lost teeth over the roofs of their houses. They wish for the teeth to be replaced with stronger ones.

In many countries, including the United States, England, and Canada, children put lost teeth under their pillows. At night while they are asleep, the Tooth Fairy is believed to take the teeth and leave money or small gifts in their place.

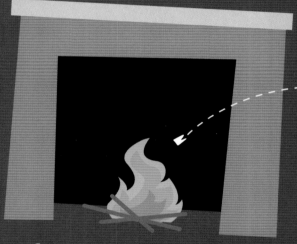

Centuries ago people threw lost teeth into fires so witches wouldn't find the teeth and put a curse on them.

Some kids put lost teeth in glasses of water, boxes, mice holes, or slippers instead of under their pillows.

In many countries, including Mexico, France, and Spain, the Tooth Mouse is believed to take teeth and leave treasures in their place.

PERMANENT TEETH

The main reason you have teeth is to chew food into tiny pieces you can swallow. Each kind of tooth has a different job.

INCISORS are the 8 teeth in the front of your mouth. They are for biting food.

CANINES are the 4 pointy teeth. They are for tearing food apart.

BICUSPIDS are the 8 teeth with 2 sharp points that crunch and shred food. Bicuspids replace primary molars.

MOLARS are the teeth at the back of your mouth. They mash and grind food into tiny pieces.

Everyone has a unique set of teeth. Just like your fingerprints, no 2 sets of teeth are the same.

TOOTH DECAY

cavity

gum disease

germs

plaque

TOOTH DECAY happens when a tooth rots. Tiny germs live in **PLAQUE**, a sticky film on the surface of your teeth. Some of these germs can rot your teeth.

The rotten part of a tooth is called a **CAVITY**. Cavities can cause toothaches.

GUM DISEASE is when germs rot your gums. The gums become red and sore. Without healthy gums your teeth could fall out.

A long time ago it was thought that toothaches were caused by a worm, called the toothworm, that ate away at the inside of teeth.

In ancient Egypt it was believed that a freshly dead mouse applied to a toothache would cure the pain.

George Washington had bad tooth decay. Over time all his teeth were removed. A false pair was made from ivory, gold, human teeth, and animal teeth. Metal springs held the teeth together. This may be why Washington didn't smile much.

In Europe during the Middle Ages it was believed that kissing a donkey could relieve a toothache.

BRUSHING

The most important thing you can do to protect your mouth from tooth decay and gum disease is to keep it clean by **BRUSHING** with toothpaste and a toothbrush. Brushing cleans away food and plaque that sticks to your teeth and gums.

HOW TO BRUSH

1 Squeeze this much toothpaste on your toothbrush.

Soap and chalk were once ingredients in toothpaste.

YUCK!

2 Gently brush your teeth with small round strokes. Start from the back of your mouth and work your way around to the other side.

RIGHT

DO NOT

brush with up-and-down strokes because it can harm your gums.

WRONG

Make sure to brush all your teeth on all sides.
Brush for 2 to 3 minutes.

NEXT STEP

3 Spit out the foamy toothpaste into the sink.

4 Rinse your mouth out with water until all the toothpaste is washed away.

Brush your teeth **2** times a day—once after breakfast and once before you go to bed.

Crocodiles let birds pick their teeth clean.

GROSS!

The ancient Romans mixed ground-up bones, eggshells, seashells, and honey to make toothpaste.

Toothbrushes were once made from hog and cow hair.

Flossing

Dental Floss

Another important step in keeping teeth and gums healthy is **FLOSSING** with dental floss. Floss is a small thread you put between your teeth to get rid of food and plaque your toothbrush missed. You should start flossing as soon as your teeth are touching each other. Floss your teeth every night before bedtime.

Dental floss and toothpicks were used by cavemen. Scientists have discovered them in the grooves of their teeth.

DENTIST VISITS

A **DENTIST** is a doctor for your teeth. He or she will check for cavities and gum disease and will repair any decayed or damaged teeth you might have.

The dentist will take photos called **X-RAYS** of your teeth to look inside them for any decay.

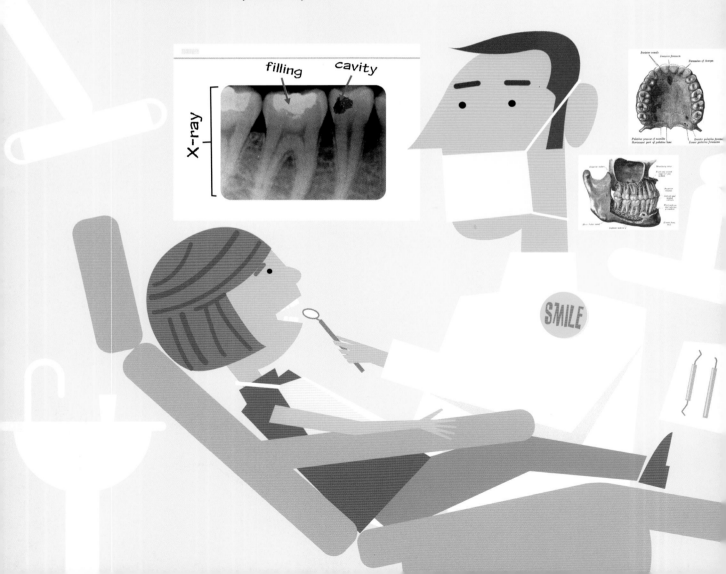

filling

cavity

X-ray

SMILE

If you do have a cavity, the dentist will remove it. But first, he or she will place some special medicine next to your tooth. The medicine numbs the tooth so you won't feel any pain.

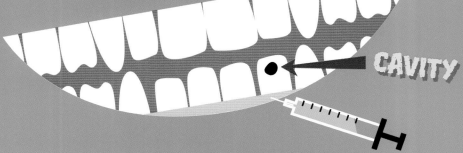

CAVITY

Once the medicine goes to work the dentist can remove the cavity with a small electric **TOOTH CLEANER**.

A small hose sucks away liquid in your mouth so you don't drool.

When the cavity is out, the dentist fills the hole with a paste called a **FILLING**. The filling will quickly harden so you are ready to bite again.

Filling

Back in the 1200s, before there were dentists, barbers removed rotten teeth.

THERE'S MORE

A **DENTAL HYGIENIST** is a professional who will give your teeth a really good cleaning using special tools. The hygienist can teach you how to brush and floss correctly.

To keep the teeth and gums in tip-top shape, it's necessary for most kids to visit the dentist and hygienist **2** times a year.

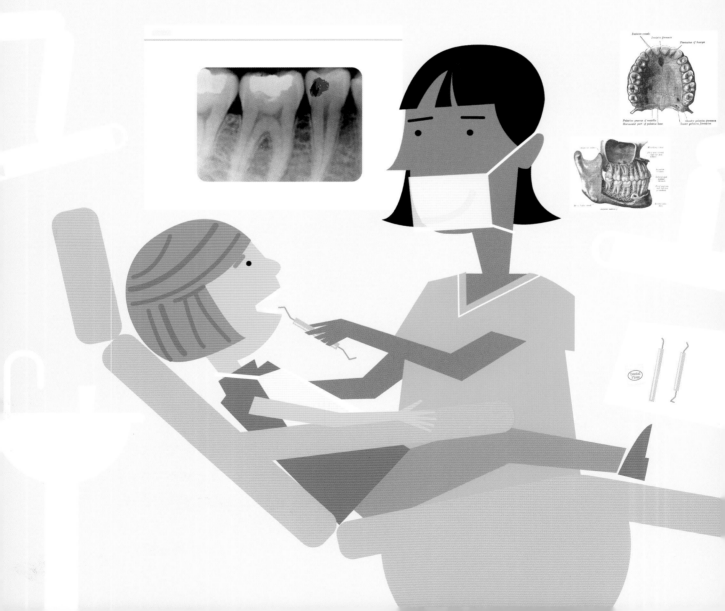

EAT RIGHT

Eating good food promotes healthy teeth and gums. **VITAMINS** and **MINERALS** found in the right foods help make teeth strong and able to fight off decay.

VITAMIN B

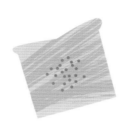

is found in whole grain breads and cereal. It's important for healthy gums.

VITAMIN C

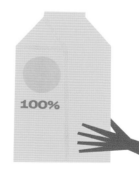

comes in oranges, grapefruits, and 100% fruit drinks. It helps fight off germs that cause tooth decay and gum disease. However, juice has natural sugar in it, so don't sip it all day.

MORE GOOD STUFF ➜

CALCIUM

is a mineral found in milk, yogurt, cheeses, and green vegetables. It helps make your teeth strong.

FLUORIDE

is a mineral that protects teeth from decay. It's sometimes added to water and is an ingredient in toothpaste.

TOOTHPASTE

SUGAR is BAD for your

teeth. When germs in the plaque on your teeth feed on sugar, acid forms. The acid eats at teeth and causes tooth decay. Sugar is found in candy, cookies, cakes, chocolate, ice cream, gum, soda, and sweet drinks. You should not snack on sweets very often, and you should brush after you eat them.

Queen Elizabeth I had rotten teeth because she ate lots of sugar cubes.

FIRST AID

TOOTHACHE:

1. Rinse your mouth out with warm water to remove any food pieces.
2. Don't eat very hot or cold foods.
3. Call the dentist for advice.

KNOCKED-OUT PERMANENT TOOTH:

1. Do not touch the root of the tooth.
2. Rinse away any dirt from your mouth with milk.
3. Reinsert the tooth if possible. Hold it gently in place with your finger.
4. If you can't reinsert the tooth, place it in milk.
5. Get to the dentist as quickly as you can and bring the tooth.

BROKEN TOOTH:

1. Save the broken pieces.
2. Rinse your mouth with warm water.
3. Don't eat hard foods.
4. Call your dentist for an appointment.

BLEEDING GUMS:

1. Rinse your mouth with warm salt water.
2. Make an appointment with your dentist for an exam and cleaning.

SAFETY

A mouth guard is a soft piece of plastic that fits into your mouth around your teeth while you play sports. It protects teeth from injury—just like a helmet protects your head— in case you fall, get elbowed in the mouth, or get hit by a ball.

THE DON'TS

DON'T bite hard objects such as pencils, rulers, and hard candy. You could damage your teeth and gums.

DON'T run with objects in your mouth. If you fall you could damage your teeth.

DON'T clench or grind your teeth. You could wear away the enamel that protects them.

DON'T run on stairs and do hold onto handrails.

DON'T shove or push someone.

DON'T leave toys where you or someone else could trip over them.

DON'T consume too many foods or drinks with sugar in them.

DON'T bite your fingernails.

OUCH!

HEALTHY TEETH & GUMS

1 Brush your teeth twice a day with a soft bristle toothbrush.

2 Floss between your teeth before bedtime.

3 Replace your toothbrush every 3 months.

4 Visit your dentist as often as he or she recommends—at least 2 times a year.

5 Eat the right foods.

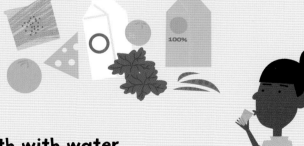

6 Brush or rinse your mouth with water after you eat sweets and chewy fruits.

The best thing about healthy teeth and gums is a nice,

BIG,

happy

smile.

WEBSITES

Montefiore Medical Center
Pediatric Dentistry
http://www.montefioredental.com/mdd-pediatric__dentistry.htm

American Dental Association (ADA)
National Children's Dental Health Month
http://www.ada.org/prof/events/featured/ncdhm.asp

American Dental Association (ADA)
History of Dentistry
http://www.ada.org/public/resources/history/index.asp

Toothfairys.net
Tooth practices around the world
http://www.toothfairys.net/usatoothfairy.htm

Copyright © 2008 by Edward Miller III
All Rights Reserved
Printed and Bound in Malaysia
www.holidayhouse.com
10 9 8 7 6 5 4 3 2

Library of Congress Cataloging-in-Publication Data
Miller, Edward, 1964—
  The tooth book : a guide to healthy teeth and gums / by Edward Miller.—1st ed.
    p. cm.
  ISBN 978-0-8234-2092-6 (hardcover)
1. Teeth—Care and hygiene—Juvenile literature. 2. Gums—Care and hygiene—Juvenile literature.
    I. Title.
RK63.M53 2008
617.6'01—dc22   2007018302

  ISBN 978-0-8234-2206-7 (paperback)

The art for this book was created on the computer.
Book design by Edward Miller.

Many thanks to Dr. Steven Chussid,
D.D.S., Director of Pediatric Dentistry
at Columbia University School of
Dental and Oral Surgery, for sharing
his expert knowledge of dental care.
—E.M.

Dental Floss